Financially
Fit

How to manage your money, get out of debt, build wealth, and *enjoy the ride*!

A Three-Part Series

Book One: How to Cure Money Stress

What you can learn from others mistakes

By

Dr. Tony Pennells M.B.B.S, Dip. FS

By the Author
Dr. Tony Pennells M.B.B.S, Dip. FS

ȸ

Books

Financially Fit - Book One: How to Cure Money Stress

Financially Fit - Book Two: 30 Days to Financial Fitness

Financially Fit - Book Three: Your Path to Financial Freedom

Connect with me!

I love getting feedback from my readers and would really appreciate you taking a few minutes to post your comments or a brief review on my Amazon page.

https://www.amazon.com/author/drtonypennells

Also come join our Facebook community here:
Facebook - www.facebook.com/finfitwithdrtony

Thank you!

Disclaimer

General Advice Disclaimer

This book is presented solely for educational and general information regarding the subject matter covered. The author and publisher are not offering it as financial, legal, accounting, or other professional services advice. Whilst reasonable precautions have been taken to ensure the accuracy of the material contained herein at the time of publication, no person, persons or organisation should invest monies or take action on reliance of the material contained herein but instead should satisfy themselves independently of the appropriateness of such action.

No Warranties

While reasonable precautions have been used in preparing this book, the author and publisher make no representations or warranties of any kind and assume no liabilities of any kind with respect to the accuracy or completeness of the contents and specifically disclaim any implied warranties of merchantability or fitness of use for a particular purpose. Neither the author nor the publisher shall be held liable or responsible to any person or entity with respect to any loss or incidental or consequential damages caused, or alleged to have been caused, directly or indirectly, by the information or programs contained herein. No warranty may be created or extended by sales representatives or written sales materials. Every person is different and the advice and strategies contained herein may not be suitable for your situation. You should seek the services of a competent professional before beginning any improvement program. Some parts of the story and its characters and entities may be fictional. Any likeness to actual persons, either living or dead, is strictly coincidental.

Liability Disclaimer

The publishers, authors, and any other parties involved in the creation, production, provision of information, or delivery of this book specifically disclaim any responsibility, and shall not be liable for any damages, claims, injuries, losses, liabilities, costs or obligations including any direct, indirect, special, incidental, or consequential damages (collectively known as "Damages") whatsoever and howsoever caused, arising out of, or in connection with, the use or misuse of the book and the information contained within it, whether such Damages arise in contract, tort, negligence, equity, statute law, or by way of any other legal theory.

You may *NOT* give away, share or resell this intellectual property in any way.

Copyright © 2013 by Dr Tony Pennells

All rights reserved. No part of this publication may be reproduced or transmitted in any form or by any means, electronic, or mechanical, including photocopying, recording, or by any information storage and retrieval system, without written permission from the publisher.

Published by: Doncarie Pty Ltd

Dedication

This first book is dedicated to my amazing wife, who for years has stood by my side while I made mistakes, learnt and overcame challenges along the way.
Her unwavering support, patience and belief in me has been my rock and source of inspiration.
To the love of my life, Wui Yen, you are awe-inspiring!

How to Cure Money Stress

Foreword ix

Series Introduction 1

Chapter 1 Global Unrest 32

Chapter 2 The Paradox of Wealth 46

Chapter 3 Money Mistakes 52

Chapter 4 Where is the money going? 61

Chapter 5 Government 67

Chapter 6 Myths & Truths 73

Conclusion 93

Research 98

By the Author 101

Connect with me! 104

Foreword

Thank you for taking the time to read this book. It is the first in a series titled '*Financially Fit*'.

My motivation for writing this series came from seeing thousands of people, including close friends and family, struggle with money throughout their working lives, never reaching a point of financial freedom.

At the surface it seems so simple: provide for yourself today, whilst building your wealth to a point where you are financially secure enough to support yourself for the time when you no longer want, or are unable, to work.

However, the reality is very different for most people. Very few ever achieve true financial security and the majority of the population find that "money worries" rob them of their day-to-day peace of mind.

From a young age I saw my parents struggle with this as well. Arguments over money – how and where it was being spent, and worry over whether there would be enough to last until the next payday, let alone trying to save extra for the future placed tremendous stress on their marriage. This was ultimately a major factor in their divorce when I was in my early 20s.

This shocked me.

I couldn't understand why they were not able to get this part of their lives together. It shouldn't have been that hard.

I made a commitment to myself that I would not make the same mistakes - I would have a different future.

This commitment marked the beginning of my journey to discover the differences between those that have and the have-nots, the people who *did* become financially secure versus those that *did not*.

What I discovered is that the pathway to financial security is actually quite simple. However, "simple" doesn't necessarily mean "easy". Like any fitness program, it involves re-training and discipline. For most people this means un-learning the wrong financial habits, and learning some new and effective strategies to develop financial fitness.

The great news is that just about anybody can learn these new habits, put them into action and become financially fit within just a month or two.

What I have tried to do in this series is to create a simple step-by-step "how-to" guide.

My original motivation of putting 'pen to paper' was, and still is, to produce a blueprint that my children can follow. This book provides the way forward to how they can start providing for their futures today.

The books in this series go further than just discussing the principles and values of becoming financially secure; they also offer practical tips and techniques that you are able to apply in your own life.

My wish is for you to experience the peace of mind that comes with giving yourself permission to enjoy your life now, with the confidence of knowing that you're becoming financially secure with each passing day.

Enjoy!

Dr Tony, September 2013

Series Introduction

Different Paths

How can so many people get it so wrong?

Surely it can't be that hard!

The goal seems simple enough: earn enough money to provide a comfortable life for you and your family today, and save enough to look after yourself when you are no longer working.

Did you know?

*Two-thirds of people rely on the government pension as their main source of income in their retirement. *Source – ABS*

We live in the 'luckiest country in the world', surrounded by wealth and resources,. Yet, most of us wrestle daily with financial stress, worried that we never have enough money to pay all the bills on time, or enough to last through to the next payday. The idea of putting any savings away for a far off retirement date seems like an unrealistic goal.

Did you know?

*The average income for a full-time worker in Australia is around $63,000; whilst the full government pension for a couple is less than $29,000 per year – <u>less than half</u> of what many households already find difficult to get by on. *Sources - ABS and Centrelink.gov.au*

This struggle leaves many people with no real savings. An unexpected emergency, such as a major car repair or medical bill, can be enough to tip them over the edge. An increasing number of people are borrowing on their credit cards for everyday expenses and barely making minimum repayments, let alone paying off the cards each month.

Did you know?
Only 7% of retirees are currently financially secure, and a large proportion of the population will need to live on <u>less than 40% of their pre-retirement income</u>. *Source - Australian Investment Institute, 2011

This statistic bears repeating: after more than 40 years in the workforce, less than 7% will be able to retire comfortably. When I first learned that figure, I couldn't believe it. I wondered, how could that be in this country, when people are better educated and earning more than ever before? How could 93 out of every 100 people, including our friends, family, colleagues and neighbours, be getting it so wrong?

How can you be sure that you don't fall into the same trap?

What are the 7 out of 100 people that ARE financially secure doing to get it right?

Have they spent their lives overly focused on money? Have they lived the life of a scrooge, having money, but never having enjoyed life?

OR

Do they run their financial lives with a different set of money habits and rules?

Many people want to "live life today AND enjoy a financially secure future", but don't know how to achieve that goal.

I've often heard people say:

"I'd just like to follow a plan that will give me financial security, without me having to be a financial genius or predict what to invest in and when. I'm too busy for that."

"I need a plan that I can understand, one that is tailored to me and my goals, so that I can enjoy life today and have peace of mind about my future."

The good news is that you can enjoy life today, *and* have financial security tomorrow. You can also set your plan up to run virtually automatically by following some simple rules, and having some good people around you to help you make sure your plan stays on track.

What kind of life do you want?

Let's be absolutely honest about this:

Given the choice, wouldn't you choose to be wealthy rather than poor or middle-class?

Wouldn't you love to spend without worry?

Deep down, wouldn't you love it if you didn't have to work for money, and instead work in an area that you are passionate about without any concern about how much it pays you? Wouldn't you like to retire while you are still young enough to enjoy it?

Most of us know that we need to invest our money and build it up to the point where it is eventually enough to look after us in retirement. This desire drives the culture of "one big Lottery win and I'm out of here". It also drives some people to try to pick that one miracle investment that will make them a millionaire.

The problem is that usually there is no specific plan being followed, and therefore, most people don't get the result they dearly wish for - to become truly financially independent.

Life doesn't have to be a struggle filled with ongoing financial stress, BUT you cannot simply hope that just because you work hard that somehow you will automatically waltz into financial security!

I've got a good job, and earn a good income

Just because you work hard or studied hard, got a university degree and are working in a high paying profession it doesn't automatically mean that you will become financially secure.

It is how you get your money working for you that determines how financially secure you will become.

"If it's to be it's up to me."

Make The Decision:

Financial independence begins with a conscious decision to become financially fit.

This is not just a sacrifice for today with no immediate reward.

The benefits of being financially fit are the peace of mind and confidence to enjoy your life today, with the knowledge that you are also on a solid track for a financially secure future. This is an incredible gift that you can give to yourself. Being financially fit truly allows you to relax and get the most out of today.

Where did my money go?

Have you ever asked yourself, "Hey – where did my money go?"

Do you ever find yourself using this month's income to pay last month's bills?

Have you ever wondered how you got into this position…..and more importantly how to get out of it?

For most of us, we've been sold the dream that if we just go to school, study hard, get good grades and eventually get a good job, that somehow, magically, we will end up being financially secure, or better yet, wealthy, retired young, and living a dream life. For most people this dream eventually turns into a nightmare. Most of us compromise, get into debt, and struggle just to make ends meet today, with little energy or time to think about securing our financial future. Life can just grind you down over time. It can seem easier to just compromise, give up on your big dreams and goals, and settle for mediocrity, with hope that the future will somehow take care of itself. For many, their wealth plan is a combination of hoping they'll win the lottery, or hoping that the government will look after them.

If you think that people earning higher incomes are better off, this is often NOT the case. Most high-income earners have built a lifestyle where they also spend all they earn. They're often deeply in debt, with no easy path to financial security in sight. You might say that they just have better-looking financial prison cells, where they are locked into needing to earn their high incomes. If they one day find themselves not able to go to work their financial houses can come tumbling down very quickly.

Just think of the many top-earning celebrities that have hit the news over the past few years declaring bankruptcy or other financial difficulties. Michael Jackson comes to mind – earning many millions of dollars per year but living a lifestyle where he was spending more than he was earning. The banks happy to lend him money for that lifestyle, at least for a while, but eventually they wanted their money back (sound familiar?). He had to go back on tour to try to earn enough money to pay them back, despite being in poor health. Some say that the stress of this is what eventually cost him his life!

What does it mean to be Financially Fit?

Being financially fit means that you are practicing the right habits and disciplines to be on the path to financial independence.

When I talk of someone being financially independent or wealthy, I do not talk of someone earning a high income from his or her job or career. If they stop working, this income also immediately stops. Therefore they could go from a high income to no income in one day, unless they have learnt how to replace their earned income with income that comes from investments. I also do not think of someone with a high 'net-worth' as automatically being rich. They may be, if their net-worth is made up of assets that makes them money, or they may be just-off broke if their net-worth is made up of their house that they live in, holiday home and expensive toys such as cars, jet-ski's and boats etc.

You may wonder what hope there is for you if even the high flyers can't get it right. However, it *is* possible to succeed in becoming financially independent. A small percentage of people have gotten themselves into a position where they no longer rely on the money that they earn from their jobs. They have enough income coming in from various investments to be able to pay for their lifestyle (with some surplus left over), and do not have to go to work ever again if they so choose.

These people come from all sorts of backgrounds and careers, and have a range of incomes. Despite popular opinion, they are not all high-income professions such as doctors, lawyers and accountants.

When I talk of someone being financially independent, I'm talking about a person who has enough passive income that they never need to work.

Have you ever wondered how someone else just like you - from a similar background, education and income is able to become financially independent in a relatively short period of time?

What are the differences between them and you? What do they know and what are they doing with their finances that you are not?

I'll show you exactly what those differences are in this series of three books.

Different Paths, Different Results

"Insanity is doing the same thing over and over and expecting different results." ~ variously attributed to Albert Einstein, Ben Franklin, author Rita Mae Brown, and Alcoholics Anonymous

If you change nothing about your current practice, statistics show that it is likely that financial independence will remain out of reach, and eventually you will have to learn how to survive on much less income when you are no longer working.

I would like to challenge you though, to take another path - a new path – one of new knowledge, a little discipline, and a better plan.

The goal is to follow a path that guarantees that in just one to two months you will be financially fit and beginning to build passive incomes. The goal is nothing less than creating true financial independence – to eventually have the freedom to work when you want, and where you want, and to live life on your terms.

These three books give you the tools to achieve this.

Credentials?

One of my business mentors once told me to only listen to someone who has done, or is doing what they recommend. Someone who is practicing what they preach is in a unique position to teach you from personal experience, not just from theory. There is a very big difference between theory and true practical knowledge!

Let me share a little of my background and explain what I feel qualifies me to teach.

My family certainly does not come from wealth, in fact far from it. I was born in a country called Rhodesia – some of you will know it by its current name – Zimbabwe. At the age of 5, my mother, father, two brothers and I escaped from a civil war and headed down to South Africa. We came out of the country with virtually nothing, arriving in South Africa during the height of the Apartheid era.

It was, for us, a case of 'out of the frying pan and into the fire'!

South Africa was a country in turmoil. Not only was there increasing discontent amongst the African population, but also there was huge tension between the Afrikaans and English speaking Caucasian population. Violence was escalating and personal safety was being threatened more and more frequently.

It was compulsory for children to spend two years in the army after leaving school. After just three months of basic army training they would be sent to the border to fight terrorists. At just seventeen years of age, these kids were not old enough yet to vote, or drink a beer, but were being trained to shoot guns and kill people!

It was just a matter of time until the Afrikaaner controlled government was overthrown, or the country erupted into civil war. My parent were not prepared to go through that situation again, and in particular were not prepared to risk losing a child fighting in a war they did not believe in. They had the decision to leave South Africa, and start over once again, knowing that this would mean having to rebuild the family financially all over again.

After a few years, we were lucky enough to be accepted into Australia. We arrived not knowing anyone in the country, and with only a couple of thousand dollars of savings.

My dad went back to work as a hairdresser, and my mum had to find work for the first time in many years. With two modest incomes coming into the family, we were only just able to make ends meet.

As a child, I didn't feel like I went without, but my parents were never able to 'get ahead' financially. The strain also took a tremendous toll on their relationship, ultimately ending in their divorce a couple of years after I finished high school.

Australia has been very good to us though – it gave us an opportunity to start again and build a better life– but we had to seize that opportunity. And we have.

My older brother built a very successful business that he sold and retired by the time he was forty. My younger brother is a highly successful and influential journalist with a passion for reporting on social injustice around the world. He has been the recipient of numerous awards including the United Nations Media Peace Prize, multiple Walkley Awards for excellence in journalism. In 2013 he was awarded the coveted Gold Walkley – the most prestigious journalism award in Australia.

My parents believed in the adage that a good education led to a good job, and that a good job would guarantee our financial security. They pushed me to study hard, and go to university, so that I could have opportunities that they never had.

I did study hard and fortunately was accepted to study medicine at the University of Western Australia. I had to fund myself through the six years of university. I managed this through part-time work, the incredible generosity of my future in-laws, some government support, and a student loan that took several years to pay off once I qualified as a medical doctor.

My university experience was a great time in my life, especially so because I met my beautiful soul mate, who I married in my graduation year.

During my time at university, I examined the path I was on and where I was heading.

I looked at people on a similar path to myself, but who were 5, 10, and 15 years ahead of me. I observed their physical and mental health, their relationships and how they spent their time. I realized that I didn't want to be like them. Many of them were outstanding individuals and terrific doctors who worked incredibly long hours, either arriving at the hospital or medical practice early in the morning, working until late in the evening, sometimes overnight and into the next day.

Although admirable, working that hard has personal consequences. Many suffered poor health, or poor relationships with the partner or kids, or all of the above.

Also, many succumbed to peer group pressure to drive luxury cars, live in expensive houses in expensive suburbs, send their kids to the best (and most expensive) private schools, and take expensive overseas holidays every year. Often they were in debt up to their eyeballs, forcing them to work long hours just to maintain their current lifestyle.

That was not the type of life that I wanted to live.

I realized at that point that my parents had got it wrong.

Working in a respected profession had NOTHING to do with financial success.

In many cases working in a respected profession makes you time poor. So many professionals feel they do not have the time to educate themselves financially, and instead rely on 'expert advisers' who often take advantage of financial ignorance to sell them high-commission investment products that ultimately fail, taking hard earned money with it.

To see the direction you are currently heading, have a look at colleagues or family 5, 10, and 15 years ahead of you on the same path as you do now. Overlook the apparent glamour of a job title, a nice office, or leased car, and observe their lives.

How is their physical health?
How is their mental health?
What is their family life like?
> How is their relationship with their partner?
> Do they have good relationship with their kids?

Have they got time to spend with their kids?
Do they have spare time?
How much time are they able to take off each year?
How much longer do they need to be working before they have a choice to stop?

Ask yourself if this is the type of life that you want to be building.

If the answer is yes, then you are on the right path for you right now.

If the answer is no, then you need to design a different plan.

In the words of world- renowned business philosopher Jim Rohn:

"For things to change....you need to change".

When I examined where my life was heading, I realized that what I truly wanted was to be able to choose how I spend my time, instead of being forced to work. I wanted the choice to do what I wanted to do, when I wanted to do it.

I didn't know how to achieve this until I met Kim, my first business mentor.

Kim was just turning forty and had effectively retired. He had a six figure passive income coming in from businesses and investments, whether he worked or not.

Kim crystallized the game for me. He explained that the main reason people go to work is primarily to pay for their lifestyle today, and secondly to put them in a financial position so they eventually don't have to show up for work ever again. To be able to do this, you have to build up passive incomes to the point where they are higher that your monthly living expenses. So the aim of the game is to get yourself into a position where your money is coming in without you working. When your living expenses are completely covered by your passive income streams, then you are free to choose how you spend your time. You can work if you choose, and you can choose not to work. The point is you have a choice.

When I asked Kim if he could teach me to do what he had done, his answer was "probably not"!

He said that although the principles and steps were actually quite simple, he found that most doctors he knew thought they knew everything, and questioned everything he said.

He was probably right!

I was determined to learn from him though, so I pressed further until he relented, but he had conditions. I had to promise that I would do what he said, when he said to do it. There could be no excuses.

On reflection I can see that he was very smart to do it that way. I would have been a royal pain in his neck, asking *"why, why, why"* all the time. I would have also made excuses as to why I couldn't get things done, using work as an alibi. After all I was a doctor! Surely *my excuses* were important and valid. Except, those same excuses are the reason why I was not financially successful.

So, I agreed to Kim's conditions, placing my word and ego on the line.

I did what he said, when he said to do it, and within a year I was in a position to stop working as a doctor. I had not yet replaced a medical income, but we did have passive income coming in that we could live off.

Following Kim's advice gave me what I desired most - the gift of time and the freedom to choose how to spend it.

I now have time to spend with my beautiful wife and my wonderful kids. I have the time and money to travel when I want to; to sleep in when I need to; to exercise during the week when the gyms are quiet, and importantly, time to study business, finance and investing, and learn the secrets of creating and keeping wealth.

Since I left working in the medical profession, I have helped launch numerous businesses, several of which have been recognized within the top 100 fastest growing businesses in Australia by the Business Review Weekly. My current business, *Wealth Today*, is a company that exists to 'help strengthen people's financial security'. My wife and I have acquired numerous investments including property, managed investments, businesses and other assets that generate considerable passive incomes.

I share my personal experience so that you can see that this advice *works*. I am passionate about this because becoming financially independent is so much easier than you may think. If I can do it, so can you.

Keep in mind that embarking on any course for change involves challenges and missteps.

I have made mistakes along the way. Often it felt like I was taking three steps forwards and two steps back. I have accomplished my goals by setting achievable incremental targets, admittedly not always within my time frame, but I got there in the end.

What This is Not

This book is not about fancy money tricks, short cuts, or 'get rich quick' schemes. It is also not about complicated financial strategies that encourage you to spend thousands of dollars for the 'real secrets'.

What This Is

These books provide basic financial education and teach you how to design your own financial freedom plan. They work as a financial training manual through which you can build up your financial fitness and build a successful financial future, regardless of your previous education, experience, and current situation.

I can coach you to financial fitness within one to two months, and financial security within six months, but you have to show-up for the regular workouts. How successful you become ultimately depends upon your commitment to changing your life.

The *Financially Fit* personal training program is comprised of three books:

Book One: How to Cure Money Stress

This book is an orientation.

Before commencing a training program, it can be insightful to have an understanding of what has and hasn't worked in the past. To that end, 'How to Cure Money Stress' looks at the past and present financial state of nations. It examines the strength and weakness of different financial practices, and explains how large proportions of the population and even nations fail to achieve financial security, and worse, dig themselves into deeper financial holes. Further, 'How to Cure Money Stress' discusses some common myths and misconceptions around money and finances. Overall, the aim of 'How to Cure Money Stress' is to help you recognize and diagnose poor money habits and beliefs. This awareness prepares you for the foundation principles of financial fitness revealed in Book Two, and the strategies to create lasting wealth in Book Three.

Book Two: 30 Days to Financial Fitness

In Book Two we get personal. Book Two begins with a self-assessment guide that enables you to see a clear picture of your current state.

We get into the rules of the game – the rules the wealthy play by - and we make these wealth principles second nature and natural for you by providing the structure to follow.

By the end of Book Two you will have created a simple step-by-step plan that lays the foundation to achieving financial fitness within one to two months.

Book Three: Your Path to Financial Freedom

This is where you consolidate your knowledge and practice, and extend your success by applying highly effective principles of building and protecting your wealth.

The principles from these three books offer a lifetime of financial well-being.

Your Decision

Achieving financial fitness and lasting wealth begins with a decision.

This decision is the same as the decision to become physically fit. It starts with being dissatisfied enough with your current situation to be prepared to put in the effort to make a change. An equally important part of making this decision is to have a vision in your mind as to how the new you will look. For example, when exercising the chance of your long-term success is significantly increased if you have a vision of yourself looking slimmer, perhaps more "cut" or toned, and feeling more energetic. When beginning this path, I encourage you to have a vision in your mind as to how the new "financially fit" you will look and feel. This vision will serve as a motivator to help carry you through times when you may doubt whether the pain of making the change is actually worth it.

The decision to become financially fit is only the first part. The next step is to have some clear goals, and a plan as to how you are going to reach those goals. It can also be helpful to have a 'workout buddy', someone that you trust, who will hold you accountable to your goals and be able to regularly measure and track your progress.

Once you have these steps in place, the last thing that is needed is action. The first step is the hardest, but as the old Chinese proverb says – *a journey of 1000 miles begins with a single step.*

Once you've started, don't be too hard on yourself! Just because you make the decision to become fit, does not automatically make you fit the next day. It is a process, and while the results can seem slow in the beginning, you will become fitter, and your results will begin to accelerate. Even though you may misstep, what's important is to *keep going.* If you continue, your financial fitness will improve, and you will be able to accomplish things financially that would have seemed impossible only a few months earlier.

All fitness training involves discomfort in the beginning, but once started, the feeling of empowerment that 'working out' provides is deeply rewarding. You won't be 'working out' because you need to, you'll be 'working out' because you want to.

So wherever you are right now in your financial life, you can be financially fit for life if you commit to the training.

Financial Health

So what is 'Financial Health'? Well, there are four different stages.

Stage One – Financially Fit

At this stage you have got your basic financial house in order. You are living within your means, and have enough of a cash surplus every month to reduce your debt and put extra away for your future. This is the first stage that must be accomplished before any of the other stages can be reliably achieved.

Stage Two – Financially Secure

This stage is achieved when in addition to stage one, you have an emergency cash buffer in place that is equal to at least 3 months of your monthly expenses. In addition to this you have the appropriate amounts of personal insurances in place that will look after you and your family in times of ill health or tragedy.

At this level you will have at least three months to recover from any events that may cause you to lose the income from your work or employment.

Stage Three – Financially Independent

This stage is achieved when you have an investment 'nest-egg' that is large enough to last you 25 years in retirement (from age 65 through to age 90). It sounds like that shouldn't be that hard a goal, and you are right it isn't, but less than 4% of the population actually achieve it! By focusing on getting Stage One and Two in balance first, the stage is much more easily achieved.

Stage Four – Financially Free

This stage is achieved when you have passive income coming in from your investments greater than your average monthly expenses. This level is the real goal.

When you have accomplished this, you no longer need to work for a living. At this point you are free.

Although very few people actually achieve this level in their lives, this level *is* attainable by almost anyone if they follow the basic plans taught through Stages One to Three.

The purpose of these three books is to progressively take you through each of the four stages, and finally put it all together in a complete pathway that will lead you to Financial Freedom.

The Stakes

The financial truths and principles in these books enable you to take control of your future. The alternative is to struggle financially throughout your life.

The important thing to realize is that you have a choice. People who believe or hope that governments will solve their financial problems and take care of them in older age are not only refusing to take personal responsibility for their choices and situation, but will be very disappointed at retirement.

I do not believe in passively waiting on the government or on miracles [like winning the lottery] to save us.

I believe in taking personal responsibility for your own circumstances.

Chapter 1
Global Unrest

*"Those who cannot remember the past
are condemned to repeat it."*
~ George Santayana
(Spanish philosopher, poet, and novelist)

This chapter explores the financial state of the world around us.

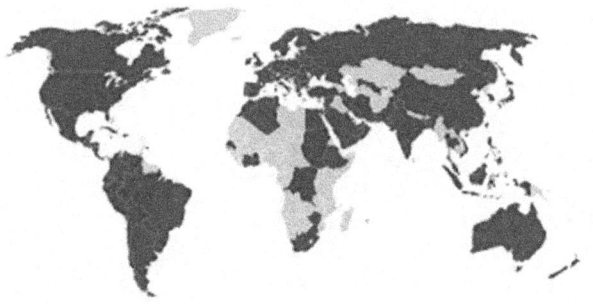

The financial condition of nations and people in most of the developed world has been declining in alarming ways. The how and why of this is relevant to understanding your financial future, because it reveals a key money secret:

Live within your means.

Between May 2012 and August 2013 the Reserve Bank of Australia dropped the interest rate six times to stimulate the growth of the economy. This apparently matters, because if the economy is not growing by at least 3% per year, the government needs to find ways to encourage hard-working people to part with their cash, even if it means they go into debt. Think about it – the reason the government drops interest rates is so that banks can offer cheaper loans, and specifically cheaper home loans.

These loans get sold to the unsuspecting public as a "buy it now" special deal, the inference being that you should lock yourself into a 25 or 30-year loan today before the interest rates go up. Low interest rates provide the incentive to get into *more* debt rather than paying back existing debt sooner.

The government does not seem to be concerned as to how you will eventually pay this money back. The emphasis is on spending to keep the economy growing – and they tell us that we all should play our part by spending and getting into debt.

This may sound cynical, but closer scrutiny reveals that the majority of governments have been and are incredibly financially irresponsible. They believe that they can keep living beyond their means and borrow money, and that somehow things would all work out.

But as we have seen over the last few years with the global financial crisis [GFC], they have got it horribly wrong, and it is the citizens who suffer.

The Global Recession

"What we know about the global financial crisis is that we don't know very much."
~ *Paul Samuelson*
(first American to win the Nobel Memorial Prize in Economic Sciences)

To keep the economy growing through the mid 2000's, people were encouraged to spend - on houses, new cars, holidays, home renovations, and plasma televisions regardless of whether they could afford it. Banks encouraged people to spend borrowed money on their credit cards by making access easier and offering higher and higher limits. Once reaching these limits, people were encouraged to refinance their home loans to clear the debts on their credit cards. Great plan! Now they had a higher amount of debt on the home loan, and meant higher monthly interest repayments. Worse, it also gave them clear credit cards to use again, reinforcing and extending their debt.

In addition, people were encouraged to buy new homes. Clever and sustained marketing sold the illusion that "they deserved it" regardless of whether they could afford it, and so many people bought homes on borrowed money that was beyond their ability to repay.

Traditionally, banks are very conservative institutions. They have strict criteria regarding who they can lend money to and how much they lend. This is important for 2 reasons: firstly, as a business they need to be sure that they can eventually get their money back. Secondly, they need to be sure that the person they lend money to can actually afford the loan – not just the repayments – meaning they can afford to repay the entire loan back in a reasonable timeframe.

Over time the banks slowly relaxed their lending criteria, allowing more people to borrow money, and borrow they did!

Through the early part of the 2000's, people spent in droves. They bought homes in their millions, to the extent that homes were being bought faster than they could be built.

Here is the important part though – because people had little or no financial education, many did not consider the purchase price they were paying for the home. Most people believed that houses were an investment that always grew in value. They failed to consider how much of their income would be taken up by the home mortgage payments, or if the home they were purchasing really was a good investment.

Millions of people began spending beyond their means!

This boom in buying demand resulted in the values of homes in the United States and many other countries growing at unsustainable rates. This growth kicked the next part into overdrive. Many people that already had homes saw the value of their homes increase, and coupled with the access to easy credit, borrowed from their homes to also go out and buy "stuff", that is, things that they wanted but didn't particularly need.

This goes against the principles of building wealth. Borrowed money, if it is used at all, should only be used to help you become stronger financially. This means using the money to buy assets or investments that can make you *more* money over time than what it *costs you in interest* on the borrowed money. What most people were doing was using the borrowed money to buy things that made them no money whatsoever, and actually went down in value over time. This unnecessary use of borrowed money made millions of people financially weaker.

It is obvious that this type of spending could not continue long-term. Two things were eventually going to happen. Firstly, people were going to run out of money and credit. Secondly, the banks were going to want their money back. When this moment came, it would come to millions of people at the same time.

The bubble finally burst in 2006. People in large numbers stopped spending money and buying homes. Many realized that they couldn't make the repayments on their loans, and stopped paying. When the banks came for their money back, people walked away from their homes, leaving them to the bank to sell. When the banks tried to sell their homes, the over-valuation of these houses was exposed. There were now greater numbers of houses for sale than buyers. With so much supply and with much lower demand, the value of houses dropped dramatically.

The banks were also in trouble. People walking away from their loans meant that the banks were not getting income from the interest payments of the original loans, let alone the original loaned money. In many cases the banks were only able to get back a fraction of the original loan amount.

If this was only happening to a handful of people, we wouldn't have felt the global effect. But as it was happening to millions of people, the dramatic drop in value of millions of loans had a global impact, causing severe damage to financial institutions around the world, which in turn led to a global recession.

This recent global recession is described as one of the worst since the Great Depression of the 1930's in the United States. Although recognized as over in mid-2009, economists predict that it will take many years before a full recovery is felt.

The Debts of Nations

When a government takes in less money than it spends it lives beyond its means and just like a person or a household, it accumulates debt.

As national debt rises, people are subjected to the threat of rising taxes as the government has to spend more and more on interest payments. Often this can result in cuts to national spending on security, health, education and infrastructure, which eventually can undermine national, social and political stability.

Case Studies:

Greece

In 2010 the world discovered that Greece was in deep financial trouble. Having spent beyond their means for many years, they had borrowed so much money over-time that there were serious doubts about Greece's ability to repay its debt. They have had to rely on hundreds of billions of dollars of bail-out money from other countries to try to avoid bankruptcy.

Greece isn't the only country in trouble.

The United States of America

$16,499,067,183,837.45

As of 14 February 2013, the gross national debt of the United States is more than $16 trillion dollars, and growing at an alarming rate of more than $3 billion dollars per day. With a population around 313,507,650 people, that's more than $52,000 for every man, woman and child in the US. As you can imagine, the national debt is a subject of heated debate among politicians and citizens in the United States.

Italy

National debt: $2,490,330,054,645

National debt per person: $40,888.95

Population: 60,933,442

National debt as % of GDP: 120.5%

Total annual debt change: -0.6%

Japan

National debt: $12,642,010,382,514

National debt per person: $100,152.73

Population: 126,226,775

National debt as % of GDP: 220.0%

Total annual debt change: 1.4%

United Kingdom

National debt: $2,162,908,196,721

National debt per person: $34,324.14

Population: 62,979,562

National debt as % of GDP: 89.2%

Total annual debt change: 10.6%

China

National debt: $1,269,034,426,230

National debt per person: $956.41

Population: 1,326,464,480

National debt as % of GDP: 15.7%

Total annual debt change: 17.3%

Australia

National debt: $394,534,426,230

National debt per person: $17,333.56

Population: 22,782,732

National debt as % of GDP: 27.0%

Total annual debt change: 6.3%

Australia's national debt has been swelling in recent years despite experiencing an economic boom in the mining sector.

This had been due to government "stimulus" spending, where they have increased their spending by far more than the increases in tax revenue that they have been receiving. This has lead to the paradoxical situation of one sector of the economy doing quite well, whilst many other areas are struggling with increasing cost of living pressures, rising unemployment and stagnant wages.

Many Aussies have been resorting to second jobs and selling things on eBay to make ends meet, barely able to afford rent, with the dream of owning their own home slipping further away. A friend of mine recently told me that she works with someone who lives in a share house where one of her roommates has just moved into the backyard of the house to live in a tent because he can't afford to pay the rent. She also said that this is now quite common.

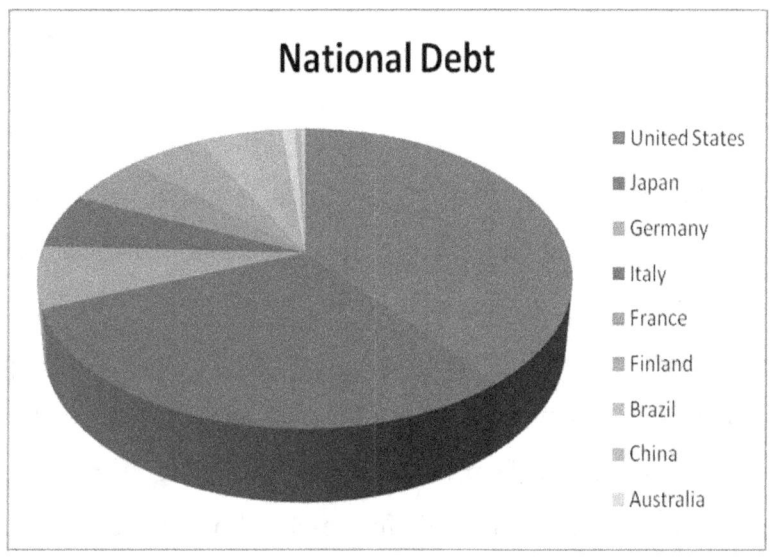

National Saving

Conversely, nations with good savings habits tend to have more surplus cash. This results in better economies and higher employment. It's simple. People or nations that have no debt do not have to make interest payments. Instead of paying interest on a debt, they have money to save or invest, from which they *earn* interest. This will generally mean that they have *more* surplus cash available to spend *today*, and if they save it, they will also have a larger amount of surplus cash in the future. Nations, such as China, that have learnt to live within their means are becoming the new powerhouses of the world. They are the ones who have the money to lend to the countries that are borrowing, and the former powerhouses are coming to them on bended knees.

Given that this seems obvious, you might wonder why so many nations live beyond their means. In my opinion, it is because in most countries the government is only in office for 3 to 4 years before they have to stand for re-election. In many cases, the problems that come with living beyond one's means will not surface in that time. Their only concern is keeping people happy today, and thus hopefully winning re-election. To that end, they lie and pretend that they can afford extravagant promises. To fulfill these promises they borrow, and encourage their citizens to borrow and also live beyond their means. Gradually saving rates decline, interest payments go up, and there is no free cash to put away for the future. In fact, the national savings rate of the United States actually dropped below zero in the late 1990's, a sure sign of catastrophe to come (and it did!).

At the time of writing, from high to low, national savings rates (outside of mandatory retirement savings) were roughly:

- 38.0% - China
- 34.7% - India
- 19.5% - Turkey
- 14.3% - Switzerland

- 12.3% - Ireland
- 11.7% - Germany
- 7.0% - United Kingdom
- 6.8% - Brazil
- 3.9% - United States
- 2.8% - Japan
- 2.5% - Australia

The nations with a high national savings rate (15% and above) are in a good long-term position. As their population ages it is unlikely that they will be depending on the government to support them. This means that the government will not need to devote large amounts of money to pensions and social security. This money can then be spent elsewhere, for example in infrastructure, health care, schooling and creating jobs.

Countries with low savings rates have big problems in the making. The opposite will be true for them. Over time they will have to spend more and more to support an aging population that are not able to financially support themselves. This will mean that they have increasing less money to spend on other important areas.

Chapter 2

The Paradox of Wealth

The financial health of nations ultimately depends on the financial literacy of its people. Improving your financial literacy benefits not just you, but also your family, your neighborhood, and even your country.

The age of the internet has moved us all next door to each other. We are no longer immune to financial problems experienced in other countries. However we can play our role in improving the whole world by putting our own financial houses in order.

Distribution of Wealth

The paradox:

80% of global wealth is held by 20% of the world's population. This is not the income people earn, but the value of the investment assets that they own.

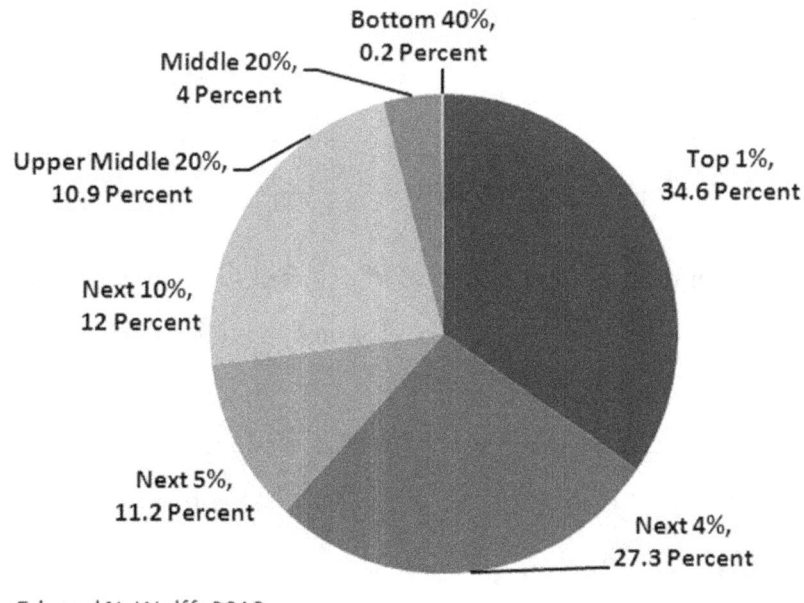

Edward N. Wolff, 2010

Throughout history, going back a far as the Roman Empire, there have been many attempts to redistribute the wealth more evenly across all levels of society. Yet despite all the efforts the wealth *always* comes back into the hands of the same few people.

The rich got richer, while the poor got poorer.

The reason for this is comes down to the *individual financial literacy* of the rich – what they know about how to manage their money, and the principles and rules that they follow. It is very obvious that what they do *must be very different* to what the poor and middle class do.

Economic Classes

In general, what are some of the differences in values and principles between the "upper class" and "middle class"?

The "upper class" generally value higher education and building and protecting wealth over a high-income job. They place a much higher priority of buying and building investment assets rather than nicer cars and homes (these come later, and are paid for by their investments, not their job income). The "upper class" understand that they need to have most of their income coming from their investments, not their job – so they make sure that their investments are *making them money now*, not waiting and hoping to make money from them at some far off future date. They also have a focus on teach financial literacy and principles to their children in the hopes of passing on and preserving the family wealth.

However, the "middle class" is more generally concerned with income they earn from their jobs. They tend to view wealth as something for retirement, or only as a buffer against emergencies and lean times. Net worth for the middle class generally includes ownership of a home as well as some planning and savings for retirement, but very little savings or other investments. The other key difference is that when they do buy an "investment" it very seldom makes a positive income for them. They tend to hope that it will eventually grow in value and they can make some money from it later – *this is categorically opposite to what the wealth do!*

So, can you move up to the next level, or are you stuck in lower or middle class?

Research shows that staying in position or moving upward is primarily dependent on a person's philosophy, or belief system.

Your beliefs organize your actions. Becoming financially fit requires you to learn strong money habits. To learn and embrace these as a way of living life, you need to examine what you currently believe around money and wealth, because it is these beliefs that have got you where you are today. More importantly, changing or discarding the wrong beliefs and adopting a new philosophy, one that is grounded in the principles covered in these books, is the key to taking back control and becoming financially fit for life. To achieve this, you begin by improving your financial literacy.

Financial Literacy

"There's nothing more expensive than poverty."
~ Ellis Yochelson
(Johns Hopkins University Professor)

Financial illiteracy has negative effects throughout one's entire life. People who are more money-savvy are more likely to plan for retirement, and according to one study, people who plan for retirement have twice the net worth of people who do not.

Those not financially educated have been shown to suffer more, borrow more and pay more in fees and interest rates.

Conclusion

The financial health of nations and of the world is actually the collective financial health of individuals. Financial education is sorely lacking in most modern education systems, to the detriment of us all.

So as we are often left to provide our own financial education, many remain financially illiterate and suffer the consequences, as proven by the alarming financial state of nations.

You can change that. Your individual fate lies in your hands. By understanding how the belief system of the wealthy differs from the middle class, you can learn and apply their principles and rules, and experience the same results for yourself.

Chapter 3
Money Mistakes

"Knowledge is power."
~ Martin Luther King

Learning and knowing how money works is the first step in successfully handing one's financial affairs. This not only allows you to avoid financial hardships, but also to develop financial fitness and ultimately financial independence and freedom.

The previous section provided a global orientation. This section focuses on individual financial performance (or the lack of it) and the correlation to financial literacy.

"My father said in the 1920s his math classes included a lot of following the stock market, filling out practice tax returns, and problems involving banking decisions. He was surprised that my classes included none of that and I had never taken economics."

~ blog post

Financial Literacy

What does "financially literate" mean? A "financially literate" person would have knowledge, skills, and confidence to manage even limited financial resources effectively and be able to create a lifetime of financial well-being. He or she will be familiar with basic financial terminology and be able to reasonably predict the outcomes of financial decisions.

Predictors of failure

If you take the time to step back, you can quite clearly see the indicators that someone is on the path to financial failure, or at best, a life of financial struggle.

Have a look at some of these facts below and see what you think:

Education

Surveys show that less than 10% of American high-school graduates were given even basic personal financial education.

Perhaps even more alarming, many people surveyed regarded themselves as financially knowledgeable even though their behavior indicated that they neglected or were ignorant of basic mathematical comparisons that would have led to better financial decisions.

Income

Roughly 75% of Americans live "month-to-month" financially, or "hand-to-mouth."

No matter how much people earn, they are increasing their monthly expenses and continuing to live at or beyond their means.

Almost half of the people in a recent survey reported having difficulties simply paying monthly expenses. They are consistently not able to save part of what they earn for their future needs.

Budgets

Most people do not know how to use a budget, or the purpose of a budget. A budget is simply a way for you to see where you can find savings. Once these savings are found, they can be used to pay yourself first - by regularly putting money away for your future. This is the key to financial security - making your money work for you, so that eventually the income from your investments is more that your monthly expenses.

Debt

"Neither a borrower nor a lender be, For loan oft loses both itself and friend, And borrowing dulls the edge of husbandry." ~ *William Shakespeare (Hamlet Act 1, scene 3, 75–77)*

The amount of credit card debt held by college students has been rising steadily in recent years, and at rates of growth exceeding 46%.

The average student loan debt at the time surveyed was $23,186. Roughly 40% of college grads described the debt they left school with as "unmanageable."

Student loan debts have now exceeded one trillion dollars, surpassing even unsecured credit card debts and automobile loans.

39% of us carry credit card debt, and this number stays almost the same year after year. This suggests people are generally not paying off their credit cards and paying their monthly living expenses with them.

Roughly 20% of respondents in a survey admitted to using non-bank, high-interest borrowing such as pawn shops and payday advances, and displayed little knowledge about those products such as interest rates and terms.

43% of those who lent money to family or friends were not yet paid back in full and 27% had yet to receive anything toward repayment of the loan.

Credit

56% have no idea what their current credit score is, despite this being one of the largest factors in securing a home mortgage, car loan, competitive interest rates, or even gaining employment.

We spend more when we use credit cards. McDonald's stated that when they started accepting credit transactions, the average sale rose from $4.50 to $7.00. Even if people pay their entire credit card balance every month, it has been shown they spend 12% to 18% more when using them versus cash.

32% of all US home loan applications were rejected last year, demonstrating either tightening mortgage criteria which helps slow the economy, falling applicant credentials, applicants still seeking to live beyond their means, or all of the above.

More than half of all the citizens of the US have at least one credit card, and this number is growing, indicating continued use and access of extra credit cards, despite the financial lessons we should have all learned by now.

The average credit card debt in American households was over $8,000.

Savings

Roughly 25% of Americans have no savings at all.

50% of us have less than one month's income saved.

50% of Americans saved nothing – zero – last year.

30% have less than $1,000 in total cash, in all bank accounts, at any given time.

A majority of Americans do not have an adequate cushion for emergencies and have not planned on major events like college expenses for children, medical expenses, or their own retirement.

40% of us are saving less than we did last year. This is not savings for retirement but rather a simple emergency fund. I would recommend that at an absolute minimum, you have three months, and preferably one year's worth of expenses set aside in a financial buffer account.

Retirement

For the next nineteen years, more than ten thousand people will reach the retirement age of sixty-five each and every day.

In America, social security is feared to go bankrupt in coming years.

35% will depend on social security alone, which generally pays far less than what you need to live a modest lifestyle in retirement.

30% admit to not having saved anything at all toward retirement.

60% admit they have no idea how much they will need to retire at their current standard of living.

Some estimate only one-third of adults born between 1946 and 1964 are saving enough for retirement.

At present, of this one-third, only 5% have enough saved for retirement.

Of those who do have a retirement plan set up (e.g. a 401 (k) in the USA or superannuation in Australia), only 11% are saving enough to adequately provide for retirement.

Consequences

Thirty-two million people face possible bankruptcy this coming year - more than the total number expected to graduate college. The number one cited cause of divorce in the United States is "money."

"Money" is a top-cited reason for suicides.

More and more college graduates and adults are moving in with their parents. The "multi-family" or "multi-generation" living arrangement is becoming more common.

Surveys and tests indicate a direct relationship between growing financial illiteracy, increasing consumer debt and the growing number of bankruptcies.

More people are uncertain as to how they will be able to fund their retirement.

Can you see how people do not have a clear plan or path to becoming financially secure? Most people are focused on getting by today, with virtually no real effort or understanding as to the fact that their future is entirely depended on the quality of the decisions that they are making right now.

Chapter 4

Where is the money going?

*"I'm living so far beyond my income
that we may almost be said to be living apart."*
~ E. E. Cummings

Spending

A huge number of people spend beyond their means. It has been estimated that as much as 40% of Americans will spend 110% of their income this year.

So what are people spending their money on? This chapter examines where money is going and how this has changed over the past 60 years. The following graph charts where Americans spend their money:

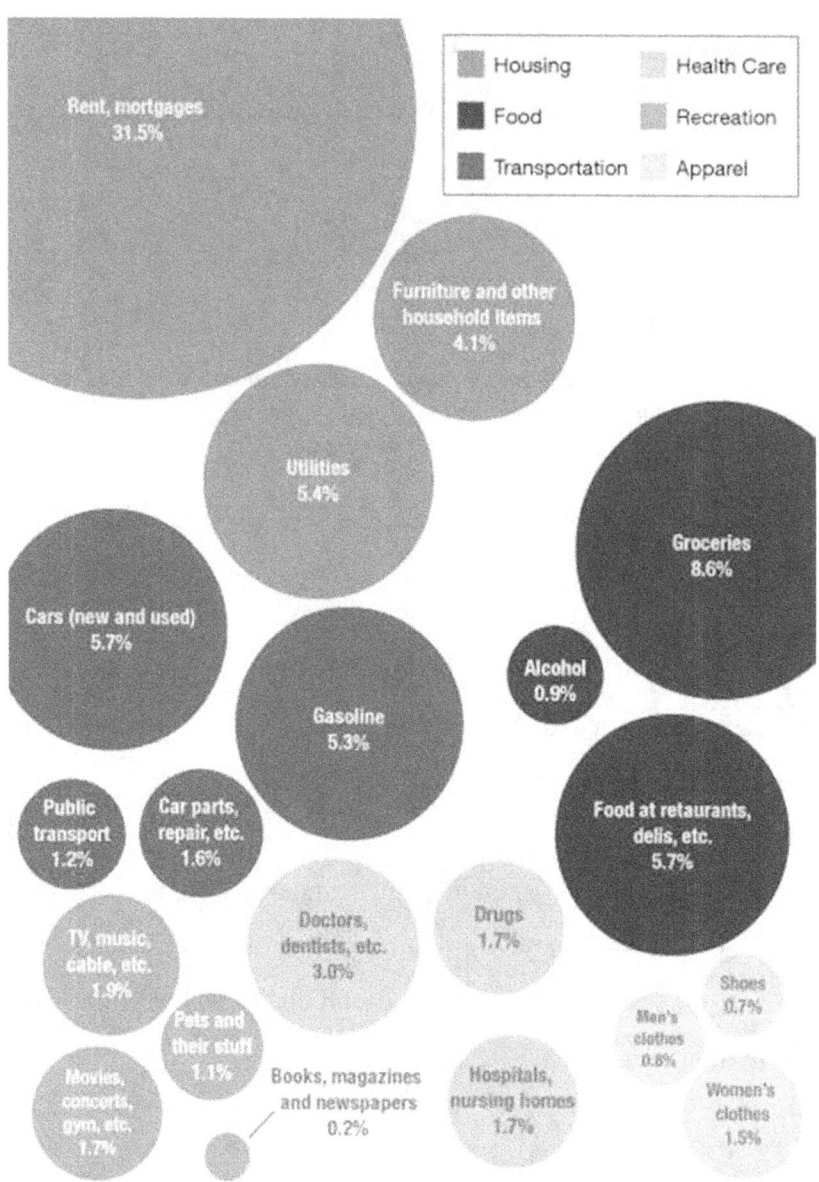

Take look at the previous image and consider where people are currently spending their money. What categories do they fit into?

As you can see, housing costs use up the bulk of income, followed by transportation, groceries and eating out.

How do you compare?

It would be useful at this stage for you to track all your spending for at least one full month, so you can construct a similar graph. This graph will give you a clearer view of your current situation, and enable you to identify possible areas for savings.

How has this changed over the years?

It is easy to think that what we spend our money on is 'normal'. Our friends and neighbours are likely to be spending in the same way. Television shows and advertisements encourage us to spend by convincing us that we really *'need'* certain items. However, the way we spend today is not 'normal'. Consider what has changed over the past 60 years through the following image:

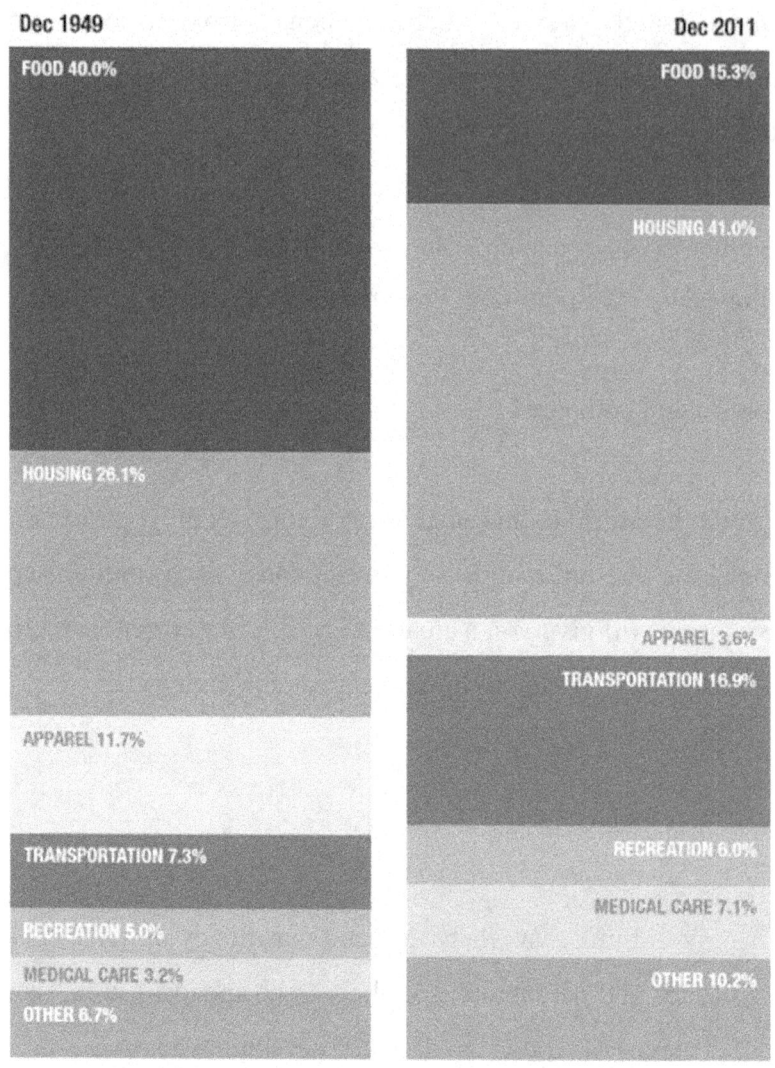

Notice that the cost of housing has gone up from 26% to 41% of total expenses. That is an increase of 15% of total expenses. Also look at cost of transportation - increasing from 7.3% to 16.9% of total expenses.

The rise in transportation costs means that this expense has grown relative to income, while the relative cost of food has gone down. Medical care has doubled. You could suspect that this is from cheaper food; however that is the subject of another study.

The biggest change over the last 60 years will be found in the finance costs. This shows that 60 years ago people didn't go into debt as easily. The banks didn't lend money anywhere near as freely, and when they did it was in much smaller amounts, and had to be paid back much quicker.

This meant that people saved and paid cash for most things in their life. This included saving to buy houses for cash, or very small loans paid back in a couple of years. Cars, where they could be afforded, were also saved for and bought for cash.

The banks only relaxed their criteria in giving out loans in the 1990's – and boy has that changed things a lot.

The change in housing costs (from 26% to 41% - *up by almost 60%*) is due to paying finance costs, i.e. loan payments.

Similarly, the change in transportation costs (from 7.3% to 16.9% - *up by over 130%)* is also almost all due to the cost of car loan repayments.

This state of affairs is our choice. We chose to get these loans, and we can choose to get out of them. Whilst paying off our debts may be initially painful, the cash that it frees up is staggering.

Imagine that you had an extra 25% of your income available to you each and every month. For example, if your household income was, say $50,000 per year, you would have $12,500 free cash to put towards becoming financially fit and secure. An income of $100,000 would equate to $25,000 free cash! This is one of the key purposes of these books - to free you from debt so that you can consciously start designing a better life.

Chapter 5
Government

"Dependency is death to initiative, to risk-taking and opportunity. It's time to stop the spread of government dependency and fight it like the poison it is."
~ Mitt Romney
US Presidential nominee 2012

How confident are you that your government will help you in retirement? Is that the proper role of government? If a government pension is your fallback position, I suggest you make other plans.

In Australia, for example, an aged pension has underpinned retirement since the early 1900's. For many, this has been the centerpiece of a "three-pillar" approach to retirement:

1. Age pension
2. Employer superannuation (or 401k) contributions
3. Voluntary superannuation (or personal retirement contributions) and other savings.

"Superannuation" refers to the Australian government's plan to collect annual contributions from workers and employers (taxpayers) in order to provide retirement funds to retirees who reach a certain age and other criteria. Employers are currently required to pay 9% (rising to 12% over the next few years) of an employee's salaries and wages into a fund, but people are encouraged to put aside even more.

Many have come to expect the above three-pillar strategy to always be available for an adequate retirement, but there are big problems with this theory.

First Problem

First, the amount of the pension is currently set at around 27% of average worker earnings. This means that in retirement you have to find a way to survive on just over *one quarter* of the income that many people already find difficult to live on today.

Think about that. How likely will retirees be able to maintain a reasonable lifestyle?

Many people reach retirement only to realize that they have squandered their forty-plus years in the workforce, along with their chance to set up a comfortable retirement.

Second Problem

The second problem is the ageing population. As of 2012, there are more people retiring than there are young people entering the workforce. The government does not have savings set aside to pay for pensions. It is instead paid from the taxes it collects from people who are working today.

As the number of retirees outpaces the number of taxpayers, the tax burden on workers grows, and the amount available for retirees shrinks – even if they have paid into such a system throughout their own careers.

What does this mean?

The government must - and is – finding ways to pay less money to fewer people, and for shorter amounts of time.

The examples are everywhere. In Australia, the required age for women to access the pension has increased to the same as the age required for men. The retirement age is gradually increasing to sixty-seven, and we can expect that to go even higher in the future. Compulsory employer superannuation contributions are already being increased from 9% to 12% by 2020. The government is not interested in whether or not you can retire comfortably – it just doesn't want to have to pay you a pension. These retirement contribution amounts are set-up to ensure *that you do not qualify* for government assistance in the future.

It is now more difficult for people with greater assets to qualify for the pension in retirement, and incentives are being put in place for both employers and workers to encourage people to stay in the workforce *even longer*.

So what does all this mean for you?

Expect Less or Plan More!

Basically, it is not the government's job to look after your retirement. In fact, to put it bluntly, the government does not want and cannot afford to pay your pension.

The government wants you to work longer and pay more taxes, increasing both your contributions to the country, to your superannuation (in Australia), and to the retirement of *others*, with blind faith that others will then fund your own retirement.

The government pension should be considered at best a fallback plan.

I predict that in the future:

1. You will need to be older to access it
2. It will pay you less in real dollars
3. It will be harder to qualify for.

It is a much safer decision for you to plan to fund your own retirement.

Chapter 6
Myths & Truths

"Be careful to leave your sons well instructed rather than rich, for the hopes of the instructed are better than the wealth of the ignorant." ~ Epictetus

Becoming *financially fit* is about earning enough for you and your family today, while putting away enough money to become financially independent over time.

However, as discussed at the beginning of this book:

"Only 7% of retirees are currently financially secure, and a large proportion of the population will need to live on less than 40% of their pre-retirement income.

This means that 93% of people are doing it wrong, and only 7% are getting it right.

So what are the 7% doing that the 93% are not?

Good question. In Book Two – 30 Days to Financial Fitness, we dive right into heart of the specifics of the success principles and rules, however there is further value to be learned from looking at others mistakes.

We've previously discussed philosophy or beliefs around money and wealth and how these beliefs will ultimately determine whether we become financially secure or not. We will now look at some common beliefs and attitudes and discuss whether they are actually myths or truths. As we work through this, think about whether any of these beliefs apply to you, and whether they may in part be holding you back.

Myths and Truths

Myth:

"The money you earn is to provide for today."

Truth:

The money you earn is actually to provide for your life today *and your future*. Without also putting some money away to provide for your future, you will always be trapped into working to earn money for today.

———

Myth:

"It's okay for your wealth to be tied up in your house."

Truth:

In short, the answer is no, it's not ok.

I do believe in owning your own home, and I definitely believe in paying off any debt on your home as soon as possible. However owning your own home will not make you financially independent.

At this point I want to touch on a new concept – Lifestyle assets and Working assets (I go into much more detail in Book Three). Lifestyle assets are things that you own that you use for your lifestyle today, such as your car, furniture in your home, and your home itself. Working assets are things that you own that you send out to work for you. The job of these assets is to grow in value, or to generate an income, or both.

The game is to get enough (working) assets to make you enough income to cover your expenses, which then gives you the choice to work, or not.

A family home is generally not a working asset. It is almost always a lifestyle asset. Even if you own your home outright, with no debt on it, it still does not make you an income.

Another problem with tying equity to your house is that should you have to sell it urgently, the process takes time, and further, you still need to live somewhere. Often, when people downsize to free up cash, very little of this cash ends up being used for investing in working assets. Or they downsize to a smaller home or apartment in a nicer and more expensive area, with very little money being left over after they have changed homes. This matters in the later stages of life, when cash is needed to buy into a retirement village, nursing home, and to afford quality healthcare. These funds are difficult to access if tied up in a home's equity.

So, becoming financially fit and ultimately financially independent requires you to do two things: pay off the debts you have, including the debts on your family home; and save money to get working assets. How to do this will be covered in Books Two and Three.

Myth:

"When I get older I will be spending less."

Truth:

There are two parts to this that may be true: If you have paid off your debts you will no longer have loan repayments to make every month. This obviously will be a huge weight off the shoulders of most people. Our goal in this program is to get you to be debt free as soon as possible and to use the extra cash to add to your investments. The second thing that generally happens as you get older is that your kids grow up and eventually leave home (although the kids these days tend to be staying at home until quite a bit older). There is no doubt that our kids are a huge expense, and it does make a big difference when they are eventually able to financially stand on their own two feet.

But outside of these two areas, this myth is not true.

First realize how much more free time you will likely have on your hands in retirement. More time to socialize, eat out, play golf, travel, etc. When considering this, many are instantly alarmed and realize money – in fact *more* money – would certainly be nice to have to go with all that extra time!

Many, if they are brutally honest, will agree that their probable period of good health will be short, and they – if they are like most retirees – have dreamed about travel in their golden years. You may have a small window of time to travel with, and this takes even more money than you probably spent and lived on as a working adult.

Further, a comfortable existence in a retirement village with any kind of amenities usually involves large monthly dues. Even if one stays at home, health care expenses usually sharply increase in our later years. Even if one is agreeable to the nursing home option, good ones can be prohibitively expensive to say the least!

Myth:

"Money doesn't make you happy." Or *"I'd rather be happy than rich!"*

Truth:

This one you have probably mulled over already, and most people like to amend the statement, or even joke around with it by stating something like, "Well it does help!"

Obviously, were you to die a lonely, bitter, cynic; hugging great mounds of gold and silver, most would agree that such was not a worthy life. Having money certainly doesn't guarantee you happiness. The reality though is that a lack of money is a major cause of stress and almost certainly guarantees you unhappiness!

What I can categorically say is that most people experience more peace of mind if they know that they are financially secure.

Myth:

"I shouldn't take a raise in pay because I'll be paying more in taxes."

Truth:

You should not ever limit yourself from earning more unless there is the unusual circumstance where less pay gives you more life choices.

But beyond even that, most tax systems are "marginal," meaning if, for example, you get taxed at 15% up to $30,000 in income and 25% above that, and you get a raise to $35,000, the first $30,000 is still taxed at 15%. It is only the new $5,000 that is taxed at 25%.

The key point here is that you still end up with more money in your pocket after you've paid the extra taxes, then what you had before… And that's a good thing!

———

Myth:

"Rent is money wasted." And "Owning a home is the best investment."

Truth:

Many people believe that they should own their own home no matter what. I must admit that I certainly am a believer in owning your own home – but not at all costs.

The problem is that most people do not consider how much owning their own home will cost them in terms of reaching future financial freedom before they go out and buy one. Many people only look at what the maximum amount of money the bank will lend them, and then they go out and buy the biggest and best home, using as much of the banks money as possible. This is one of the key reasons that people experience financial stress! They've bought a home that in reality is far beyond their means. They are spending far too much of their pay cheque just to pay the mortgage each month.

Many people would be far better off renting a modest home, and saving up a decent deposit or down payment, before going out and buying their home. Then, when considering what house to buy, they should make sure that the monthly mortgage payments make up no more than 25% of their income, and plan to pay the loan off as soon as possible.

———

Myth:

"I don't have enough money to start saving or investing."

Truth:

It actually starts with a decision to pay yourself first – before you pay any other bills. You then just have to learn to live on the remainder of what is left after you have paid yourself.

If you believe in paying yourself last – that is *after* you have paid for rent, groceries, entertainment, etc, you will generally *never* have enough money left over to save.

Think about it. For most of us we are earning more now than what we were a few years ago, and quite a bit more than when we got our first jobs. Yet when we were earning less we were still able to afford the essentials for life. We were able to afford to eat, keep a roof over our head and clothes on our back. The price of essentials hasn't changed that much. What has changed is that we have found other things to spend our money on that we now think of as essentials, but in many cases they are wants (things we want but truly do not *need*).

If you decide to pay yourself *first*, that is to put the amount for saving away the day your pay cheque arrives, no matter what, you will generally find that you will adapt your spending to the amount of money that's left over, and within 90 days it will feel normal.

The truth is it really does not take much to start saving or investing, and a little bit on a regular basis can add up to a lot, sometimes even faster than you expect.

The real key, though, is to start forming good habits, and pay yourself first. If you saved even a small amount from each pay cheque, at the end of the first month you would be a little bit wealthier and one very important habit better off than someone who saved nothing that month.

Myth:

"Paying off my credit cards will hurt my credit score."

Truth:

This is definitely false. In fact the banks look at both the available limit on your cards, and how much you currently owe on them. They use both of these to *lower* the amount they will consider lending to you.

More importantly, not paying your credit cards off every month will cost you money in very high additional interest, and suck vital cash flow out of your budget.

Pay them completely off every month if possible and always pay them on time. If you cannot pay them off every month then you probably shouldn't have them.

Myth:

"A big advantage of home ownership is deducting mortgage interest."

Truth:

Well in Australia, where I live, you cannot deduct the mortgage interest on your home. For most people in the United States who own only a single-family home of their own they discover it makes more sense to use their standard deduction than to itemize deductions and thereby be able to write off their mortgage interest. Further, the benefit of having a large deduction is greatly reduced by paying lots of mortgage interest!

As I said before, I do believe in owning the roof over your head. I believe that it is an important part of providing confidence and stability for your family. However I do not believe that it is necessarily a great investment.

Remember that your home is a *lifestyle asset*, not a working asset. It will not put regular cash flow into your pocket, and in fact will take money out of your pocket, even if you have paid the mortgage off.

You will need investment cash flow if you want to become financially independent, AND you will need somewhere to live. Therefore a successful financial strategy will plan for both – owning the home you live in debt-free, *and* building up working assets that give you the regular cash flow you need.

When thinking in this way, it is very important that the house you choose to live in is within your means. If you have a mortgage on that house it is very important that the payments on that mortgage do not take up too large a portion of our income, and that you have a plan to eliminate that mortgage as soon as possible. I will go into this in much more detail in Book Two.

———

Myth:

"I'm too young or I'm too old to start investing."

Truth:

If you're young there is no better time to start! You have many more years of compound interest ahead of you, and this increases your chances of retiring – or at least being able to – even younger than normal. You can also start by investing even less than someone older, as you have the luxury of more time for your investments to grow.

If you are older, it's not too late! What we used to consider old is not necessarily "old" anymore. Life expectancy when social security was put in place in the United States was – you guessed it – sixty-five. Most people we're only expected to live around 18 months to two years after retirement. Today they say we should be planning to fund around 25 years of retirement life.

The reality is that you cannot change your age, you only have today, and the decisions you can make today. Any decision, backed up by action that you can take now will make you that bit stronger tomorrow.

Remember that it is a dangerous strategy to hope that the government will be able to look after us in retirement. They cannot do that now – the amounts of any pensions are really quite small and certainly not enough to fund a comfortable life – just find anyone trying to live on a government pension and ask them! As more and more of the baby-boomer generation enter retirement, the amount the government has to spend on pensions is having to be split amongst more and more people, meaning they get less and less in real terms.

———

Myth:

"Money is the root of all evil"

Truth:

Money is just a symbol of energy and comes in many different forms: dollars, lira, yen, chickens, you name it. It's a form of exchange. By itself it is inanimate and does nothing. Does it sometimes bring out the worst in people? Yes, sure.

But in such a case you are pointing to the greed and selfishness that is wrong and short-sighted, not the money. It could be argued that tremendous good is done with money every day, and I'm sure you can think of real-life, personal examples you yourself have observed. The Gates Foundation is dedicated to eliminating all disease in the *world*. That takes money!

Interestingly, this myth is really just a misquote of a bible verse, which specifies the "love of money" as the real problem.

> *"For the love of money is the root of all evil: which while some coveted after, they have erred from the faith, and pierced themselves through with many sorrows."*
> *~ King James Bible*

Myth:

"The rich just get richer and the poor stay poor."

Truth:

This is generally true, but not because of the money that they have. Rather, they have become rich, and stay rich because of their beliefs, principles, rules and habits around money management.

The truth is that if you wish to become wealthy, the power lies in your hands. You will need to change the habits that have been holding you back, and replace them with better financial habits. That will not necessarily be easy and it will not change your financial position overnight. But if you are prepared to learn the habits, apply the disciplines consistently, you *will* get financially fitter and stronger and with enough time, find yourself having built a solid financial wall around you and your family.

———

Myth:

"Save first for emergencies then pay off credit cards."

Truth:

The reality is that you need to do both. It is very important to get out of debt and starting with paying off high interest credit cards is a good place to start. It is just as important to apply the discipline of paying yourself first, and starting to save and invest. In Book Three we'll work through exactly how much, and in what order you should be paying off your debt, as well as saving for future as part of your plan to become financially fit.

Myth:

"It takes money to make money."

Truth:

It actually takes financial intelligence to make money. Without this, you can just as easily lose any money that you have – just look at how many lottery winners are dead broke within a couple of years of winning millions!

The truth is that with financial intelligence and money, you can make more money.

However how does this help you if you currently don't have any money? Well, you can feel envious of those that do have money, and say "poor me", or you can make a decision to change your circumstances.

Here is the cool part – If you make a decision to *pay yourself first*, within a very short period of time you will have some surplus money that you can send out to work for you. If you reinvest the money that it earns for you (which is actually one of the next key money principles), your money will compound in value, and you will have more money working for you. Pretty soon you will be one of those people that others look at and say 'it's okay for you, because you have money, and everyone knows that it takes money to make money!' The power lies in your hands!

Conclusion

There are many myths and false beliefs, far more than I have covered in this chapter.

Did you recognize yourself, or perhaps the advice of your parents, in any of the above myths?

In some of the 'truths' you will start to see glimpses of the differences in the principles and habits of the wealthy of opposed to the middle class.

It is important, particularly in times of change, to *"stand guard at the door to your mind"* (Jim Rohn). Bad habits – i.e. habits that do not support you, or that hold you back from moving toward your goals, are most destructive when they are hidden. By that I mean that you do not recognize that you have them. One of the first steps on a new path is to recognize which habits you need to change, and which new ones you need to learn.

I'll illustrate with a cute story:

"Two sisters are in the kitchen preparing a Christmas dinner and one sister cuts the ends off the ham. The other sister asks why. The first says she doesn't know, but mom did it that way. They go to the living room and find mom and ask her why she cut the ends off the ham. Mom doesn't know, but grandma did it that way. They find grandma and ask her why she cut the ends off the ham. Grandma tells them, why, when she was growing up the little wood-burning stove we had was too small for the whole ham, so she had to cut the ends off to make it fit."

Conclusion

"Education is the most powerful weapon which you can use to change the world." ~ Nelson Mandela

I hope I have demonstrated to you first that you are not alone by a long shot. Plenty of people end up in a financial mess. Many never get out of it. Years of repeating the same mistakes place some in a perpetual state of anxiety, poor health, divorce, and worse.

We all make mistakes. No matter how bad yours may have been in the area of finance, you can start on the path to financial fitness today, and be on top of your financial life in just one to two months.

Every mistake is a learning opportunity. It's a great exercise to study your own mistakes and the mistakes of others, evaluate them and learn from them. What could I/he/they have done differently, and what would the likely result have then been?

"Fitness" as the key term for this series was chosen carefully. If you are overweight, the potential consequences may be as serious for your own peace of mind and health as being financially "overweight," but interestingly, a lack of financial fitness may harm those around you much more than your own possible obesity.

But like a weight problem (as our analogy) it is not enough to just "work harder." To many a gym member's disappointment, they have run, lifted, stretched and sweat to sometimes little or no avail. It is only when they receive the full picture of what's needed for proper, sustainable weight loss do they make the best progress.

A holistic approach to weight loss includes exercise, nutrition, mental strength, changing bad habits such as drinking, and at least occasional visits to the doctor or other qualified professional for consultations through a weight reduction regimen.

Why should your finances be treated less seriously? In fact a financial fitness program actually works in much the same way. How many people go through all of the above to shed a few pounds but never consider the same thorough approach to becoming financially fit? Interesting, isn't it?

Many people struggle with the idea of creating a financial fitness plan and have often come to me saying:

"I'd just like a plan to follow, without having to be a financial genius or predict what to invest in and when. I'm too busy for that."

"I want a plan that I can understand - that is tailored to me and my goals, but I don't want to stress about the bills I have now. I want to still be able to enjoy my life today and relax about my future"

If this is you, then you are in the right place. If you take the time to work through this series, that is exactly what you will have by the end of Book Three.

This first book was designed to get you to stop and think – to look at what you may have considered 'normal', and to see how what was considered 'normal' spending just 50 years ago is very different to what most people think of as 'normal' spending today. To also look at the differences in the results of the habits and plans of the wealthy versus those of the middle class. Hopefully it is clear that the paths produce dramatically different results.

This book has laid the foundation that we will build on in the next two books.

Book Two covers the 4 Rules of Wealth. It also details how to become Financially Fit in 30 days or less.

In Book Three, I go into building your working assets, and put it all together with Book Two to create your step-by-step path to financial freedom.

Congratulations on taking your education seriously. I look forward to meeting you shortly in Book Two – 30 Days to Financial Fitness.

In Good Health!

Dr Tony.

P.S. – Make sure you come visit my Facebook page (www.facebook.com/finfitwithdrtony) and YouTube channel (Financially Fit with Dr Tony) for the latest tips and updates, and the chance to have your questions answered.

Research

- http://www.fixthedebt.org/the-national-debt-clock-widget?gclid=CKCVmeXotLUCFQsFnQodriEA_w
- http://au.pfinance.yahoo.com/photos/photo/-/14781935/how-australias-national-debt-stacks-up/14781952/
- http://www.news.com.au/business/federal-budget/national-debt-to-reach-1-trillion/story-fn5dkrsb-1225861074909
- http://www.brillig.com/debt_clock/
- http://business.time.com/2012/04/09/op-ed-improving-financial-literacy-is-essential-to-our-nations-economic-health/
- http://www.madhedgefundtrader.com/watch-international-savings-rates-for-market-cues/
- http://en.wikipedia.org/wiki/Great_Recession
- http://www.heritage.org/federalbudget/top10-percent-income-earners
- http://www.creativewealthintl.org/whyfinancialliteracy.php
- http://www.wealtheducationfoundation.org/default.html
- http://www.bls.gov/emp/ep_chart_001.htm
- http://huebler.blogspot.com/2008/08/hh-wealth.html
- http://www.washingtonpost.com/blogs/answer-sheet/post/the-dangers-of-not-teaching-personal-finance-to-kids/2012/06/03/gJQAZchiBV_blog.html

- http://www.washingtonpost.com/blogs/answer-sheet/post/do-americans-understand-the-debt-crisis/2011/07/15/gIQAe9q3JI_blog.html
- http://blog.credit.com/2012/04/3-scary-personal-finance-stats/
- http://www.economywatch.com/personal-finance/a-dozen-shocking-personal-finance-statistics.23-04.html
- http://archive.aweber.com/t-w-j-subs/DSvTI/h/25_Shocking_Statistics_About.htm
- http://www.frbsf.org/publications/community/review/vol5_issue3/choi.pdf
- http://www.accountingweb.com/topic/education-careers/new-financial-assessment-tool-helps-consumers-financial-health
- http://njaes.rutgers.edu/healthfinance/health-behaviors.asp
- http://www.brainyquote.com/quotes/topics/topic_hope.html#rLyasv4fJTH33DYm.99
- http://www.centrelink.gov.au
- http://www.investopedia.com/articles/basics/08/financial-myths.asp#ixzz2L5k84i24
- http://www.investopedia.com/articles/basics/08/financial-myths.asp#axzz2L5jSWgVC

To give you a look inside the next book in this series, I have included the Introduction for you to "30 Days to Financial Fitness."

Introduction

"In those days he was wiser than he is now; he used to frequently take my advice." ~ Winston Churchill

Where You Are

Welcome back to *Financially Fit*. I hope you enjoyed Book One, *How to Cure Money Stress,* but more than that I hope it left you a bit shocked at the generally poor financial condition of most people and nations.

When you realize how badly off the rest of the world really is, it can not only make you feel a little better about your own financial shortcomings and past mistakes, but can also help you realize how few people actually know and practice the rules that lead to good financial health.

This *Financially Fit* series is organized as follows:

- **Book One, How to Cure Money Stress** Understanding the past and getting you mentally aware and prepared before proceeding.

- **Book Two, 30 Days to Financial Fitness**: Handling money today; getting into a stable financial situation in the present and then gaining control. Even if you stopped after studying Book Two you would have a better understanding and more tools to be able to become financially fit than most people in the world today. Book Three however, offers much more. It gives you the tools you need for achieving true financial freedom.

- **Book Three, Your Path to Financial Freedom**: The philosophy and strategies for successful investing as well as creating new income streams and then protecting your wealth and passing it on. I also finish Book Three off with my perspective on practical answers to a number of frequently asked questions.

By the Author
Dr. Tony Pennells M.B.B.S, Dip. FS

☙

Books

Financially Fit - Book One: How to Cure Money Stress

Financially Fit - Book Two: 30 Days to Financial Fitness

Financially Fit - Book Three: Your Path to Financial Freedom

Connect with me!

I love getting feedback from my readers and would really appreciate you taking a few minutes to post your comments or a brief review on my Amazon page.

https://www.amazon.com/author/drtonypennells

Also come join our Facebook community here:
Facebook - www.facebook.com/finfitwithdrtony

Thank you!

www.ingramcontent.com/pod-product-compliance
Lightning Source LLC
Chambersburg PA
CBHW072055290426
44110CB00014B/1695